RENAISSANCE AND DISCOVERY

RENAISSANCE AND DISCOVERY

PETER
BEDRICK
BOOKS

This edition published in 2002 by Peter Bedrick Books
an imprint of McGraw-Hill Children's Publishing
8787 Orion Place
Columbus, OH 43240

Copyright © 2001 Octopus Publishing Group Ltd.

The material in this book has previously appeared in *History of the World*
(Bounty, Octopus Publishing Group Ltd, 2001)

ISBN 1-57768-953-1

Printed in China

McGraw-Hill
Children's Publishing
*A Division of The **McGraw·Hill** Companies*

PHOTOGRAPHIC CREDITS

13 (C/L) Bettmann/CORBIS; 17 (T/L) CORBIS; 18 (C) Bettmann/CORBIS; 24 (C) Archivo Iconografico, S.A./CORBIS;
31 (T/R) Archivo Iconografico, S.A./CORBIS; 36, (B/R) Burstein Collection/CORBIS; 43 (B/C) Leonard de
Selva/CORBIS; 44 (C) Hulton-Deutsch Collection/CORBIS; 47 (B/R) Bettmann/CORBIS. All other images from the
Miles Kelly Archive.

QUOTATION ACKNOWLEDGMENTS

Pages 21, 35, 39, 45 published in the *Oxford Dictionary of Quotations* by the Oxford University Press; pages 17, 25, 29, quoted
in *Millennium*, edited by Anthony Coleman, published by Bantam Press; page 11 quoted in *World Book Encyclopedia*, published
by World Book, Inc.; page 41 quoted in *The Norton Anthology of Poetry*, published by W. W. Norton and Co.

Every effort has been made to trace all copyright holders and obtain permissions. The editor and publishers sincerely apologize
for any inadvertent errors or omissions and will be happy to correct them in any future editions.

Contents

The word "renaissance" means rebirth. We use it to describe the period from about 1400 onward, which saw a rebirth of human interest in the past, especially in the great works of the classical civilizations of Greece and Rome.

The Renaissance

Many of the classical works had been lost or forgotten for centuries. Artists, architects, and writers of the 1400s rediscovered them. They learned from ancient objects and texts and developed a fresh way of looking at the world. Some of the greatest poets and painters flourished in this new atmosphere of inspiration and creativity.

Conflict and war

The new ways of thinking also led to conflict. At the beginning of the 1500s, Europe was the center of the Christian world. But within 50 years the continent had been split in two by an argument over the Christian religion. This period of division was known as the Reformation. On one side was the established Catholic church of Rome, and on the other was the new Protestant faith. The split caused arguments, wars, and massacres which are still bitterly remembered today. And all the time the Muslim empire of the mighty Ottomans in the East was growing stronger and stronger.

The age of exploration

It was the Ottoman threat that pushed European sailors into finding new ways of reaching the riches of the Far East. Muslim power blocked the land routes, so traders were forced to travel by sea. In this way began an amazing age of exploration and discovery. Europeans reached America for the first time, while others crossed the Indian Ocean. The very first round-the-world voyage was completed in 1522 by one of the ships from Ferdinand Magellan's fleet, although Magellan himself did not live to witness the feat.

Wealth and power

The opening of the New World, America, and new trade routes brought great wealth to Europe, especially from China, India, and South America. By about 1600 Europe was the richest and most powerful region in the world. Countries such as Spain, the Netherlands, and Britain were beginning to take control of empires that would continue for many centuries to come.

AD

The Renaissance began in Italy. Rome, the capital city, had been one of the main centers of the classical world. It was full of magnificent old buildings and other objects that inspired the "rebirth" of culture.

Renaissance Italy

Money was an important reason why the Renaissance started in Italy. The Italian city-states were home to many wealthy families, who were eager to pay for new paintings, sculpture, and architecture. Many of the great artists who were available to do the work lived in Italy. They made this one of the most stunningly creative periods in history.

Artists and patrons

One of the most powerful families was the Medici of Florence. The family spent huge sums on new buildings and on the work of master painters such as Raphael and Botticelli. In Milan, the Sforza family employed Leonardo da Vinci on many projects. The Este family of Ferrara paid for paintings by Mantegna and poetry by Ariosto. But the richest patron of all was the pope in Rome. A succession

Giotto, revolutionary painter, at work in Padua.	*c.* 1305
Brunelleschi's dome added to Florence Cathedral.	1436
Birth of Leonardo da Vinci near Florence.	1452
Botticelli paints his Primavera ("Spring").	*c.* 1478
Leonardo begins work on The Last Supper in Milan.	*c.* 1495
Michelangelo works on painting the Sistine Chapel ceiling in Rome.	1509
Palestrina begins career as musical director and composer in Rome.	1561
Palladio publishes his Four Books of Architecture.	1570

△ St. Peter's Church in Rome, one of the world's largest Christian churches. The top of its huge dome, designed by Michelangelo, reaches more than 390 feet above the ground.

△ *A view of modern Florence. Many of the city's finest buildings, such as the Medici Palace and Library, were paid for by the wealthy Medici family.*

△ *A close-up view of figures adorning the magnificent doors of the Baptistery, an eight-sided building on one of Florence's main piazzas.*

△ *A painting of Lorenzo de Medici. The Medicis made their money through banking in the Middle Ages. Their wealth gave them control of the city of Florence.*

da Vinci

Leonardo da Vinci was one of the great Renaissance painters. His portrait of the *Mona Lisa* is known throughout the world. Da Vinci was also a great inventor, recording ideas on subjects ranging from anatomy to geology. This is his painting called the *Head of Leda.*

of popes lavished money on works of art for their palace at the Vatican. The most stupendous of these was Michelangelo's huge fresco on the ceiling of the Sistine Chapel, completed in 1511.

Painting and sculpture

For the first time since the classical period, artists felt free to show the beauty of the human body. They were helped by two things – the old Greek ideas of proportion and perspective, and the new research on how the body worked. A nude sculpture such as Michelangelo's *David* shows a deep knowledge of the action of muscles, sinews, and bones.

Almost all medieval art had depicted religious subjects. Renaissance artists began to paint other things, such as landscapes and scenes of gods and goddesses from mythology. They also painted portraits – of their patrons and of themselves – which expressed human emotions more openly than ever before.

New buildings

As a young man, Filippo Brunelleschi went to Rome and studied the huge dome of the ancient Pantheon temple. This inspired him to design another dome, which topped the city cathedral of Florence in 1436. Many people argued that his structure, built without any frame or supports, would collapse, but Brunelleschi proved them wrong.

The Italian Renaissance architect Andrea Palladio made his buildings perfectly balanced, decorating them with temple columns and roofs.

△ *A column designed by Andrea Palladio, one of the great Renaissance architects. His buildings were designed using classical ideas.*

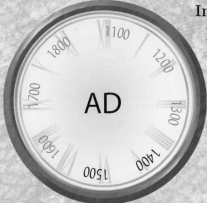

In the early 15th century, the people of Europe knew very little of the wider world. They might have heard of the adventures of travelers such as Marco Polo, but very few Europeans had gone farther afield than the Mediterranean or the Black Sea.

Exploring the World

The Muslim empires made land travel difficult beyond this region, and their merchants kept tight control of the trade routes from the East. But all the most precious goods came from the East – silks and porcelain from China, valuable spices from the Moluccas and Sri Lanka, and gold and silver from central Asia. Could European traders travel there by another route?

The route east

The answer was yes – by sea. The first to look for a new way to the East were Portuguese sailors. In 1419, Prince Henry of Portugal, known as Henry the Navigator, began sending out a series of expeditions to find a sea route around Africa. But no one knew how big the African continent was. Each ship went a little farther along the coast, and it was not until 1488 that Bartholemew Diaz sailed around the southern cape and into the Indian Ocean.

Now the route lay open to India and the Far East. In 1498 another Portuguese captain, Vasco da Gama, crossed the Indian Ocean to reach the Indian port of Calicut. He returned with a priceless cargo of pepper, cinnamon, and other goods, and a direct trading link was forged between the countries of Portugal and India. In 1514 the first Portuguese vessel sailed as far east as China.

Prince Henry of Portugal begins project to find sea route round Africa.	1419
Bartholemew Diaz rounds Cape of Good Hope.	1488
Columbus crosses the Atlantic and lands on the Bahamas.	1492
World divided between Spain and France by Treaty of Tordesillas.	1494
Cabot sails from Bristol to discover Newfoundland.	1497
Vasco da Gama sails across Indian Ocean.	1498
Columbus explores coastline of Central America.	1502
Magellan begins expedition which will eventually sail around the world.	1519

△ Ferdinand Magellan's ships thread their way through a narrow channel (later named after him) in the far south of America. They crossed the Pacific to the Philippines. Only one ship returned home, having made the very first voyage round the world.

△ *The Chinese commander Zheng-ho returned from his travels with many treasures and curiosities, including a giraffe. Chinese ships under his command visited India, Arabia, and East Africa.*

Ancient maps

By the late 1400s European scholars agreed that the world was round. The Americas did not start to appear on maps of the world until the early 1500s.

The route west

Among those who saw Diaz return from his historic voyage was a young Genoese called Christopher Columbus. He longed to see the wonders of China and Japan, and he had a surprising plan. Instead of sailing eastwards, he wanted to sail westwards right round the world to reach the civilizations in the East.

The Portuguese king would not give Columbus money for this scheme. So he went to the Spanish king and queen, who eventually gave him three ships. In 1492 Columbus and his fleet set out across the Atlantic Ocean. When they found land, Columbus believed he was near Japan. In fact, he had reached the Bahamas. He did not know that between Europe and eastern Asia was another vast continent – North America.

Around the world

Many other Europeans soon followed Columbus across the Atlantic. The fiercest rivals over trade and exploration were Spain and Portugal. To settle the argument, the Pope in 1494 fixed an imaginary line around the world from the North Pole to the South Pole, dividing the Atlantic in half. Spain could have the western half (including most of America), and Portugal the eastern half.

I believe that this is a very great continent which until today has been unknown.

CHRISTOPHER COLUMBUS, ON REACHING THE CONTINENT OF NORTH AMERICA IN 1498

△ *Early explorers navigated with the help of an instrument called an astrolabe. It was used to measure the angles of stars above the horizon.*

AD

During the Renaissance, explorers and traders found new worlds across the seas. At the same time artists found exciting new subjects and techniques, while scholars across Europe found new ways of studying human society.

Science and Technology

Scientists and inventors at this time were making important discoveries too. They were asking questions which would change our view of the earth – and the heavens – forever.

Gutenberg produces first printed work using movable type.	1454
First printing press set up in France.	1470
da Vinci designs flying machine with flapping wings.	c. 1503
Copernicus works on theory that Earth orbits the Sun (published 1543).	c. 1530
Vesalius publishes important work on the human body.	1543
Tycho Brahe begins his catalog of the stars.	1572
Invention of the telescope in the Netherlands.	1608
Galileo publishes his first account of observing the stars and planets.	1610

Printing

Throughout history, books had been rare and precious things, kept in the libraries of monasteries or wealthy houses. Each one had to be copied out by hand with pen and ink, so very few people had the chance to learn to read. The Chinese had developed a simple system of printing in the 11th century, but it was only in about 1450 that a German named Johannes Gutenberg built the first true printing press.

Using movable metal type, Gutenberg was able to make exact copies of books very cheaply. The first books he printed were the Bible and other religious works. Soon other printers started, and by 1500 they were producing many different sorts of literature, including poems and stories. For the first time, books were available to everyone.

Astronomy

In classical times, an astronomer named Ptolemy had said that the Earth was at the center of the Universe. It stayed still, while the sun and all the other heavenly bodies moved around it.

▷ Gutenberg built his press in Mainz, Germany. His metal-working skills may have come from his uncle, master of the local mint.

△ Galileo Galilei was both an astronomer and a physicist. His observations about the heavens helped to confirm the ideas of Copernicus.

△ Galileo's telescopes were more powerful than any that had been used before. He was the first person to study the night sky through a telescope.

△ Copernicus' view of the universe. He proposed that the sun, not the earth, lies at the center of the universe. He developed the idea in a book On The Revolutions of the Heavenly Spheres.

da Vinci inventions

Throughout his life, Leonardo da Vinci drew many designs for flying machines. Among these was a kind of parachute and a helicopter with spinning blades. The first successful aircraft did not fly for another 400 years.

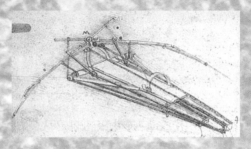

This theory became an important part of the Christian faith and of the way medieval people saw themselves. But in 1543 a new theory appeared which shocked and angered Church leaders.

According to the Polish astronomer Nicolaus Copernicus, it was the sun − not the earth − which was at the center of the Universe. The earth and other planets simply revolved around it. His idea was proved correct in the 1620s, when the Italian Galileo Galilei used an early telescope to observe the planet Jupiter. He could clearly see that there were other moons in orbit round Jupiter. Here were bodies which were not moving round the earth. This meant one thing: that the earth was not the center of the Universe.

Medicine

Doctors of the Renaissance made a much closer study of the human body than ever before to find out how it worked. They began to dissect (cut up) corpses, something which the Church had always considered sinful. The doctors described what they saw − organs, muscles, blood vessels, and bones. This helped them to discover new ways of treating injuries and disease.

Most of the important medical discoveries at this time were made in Italy and Spain. Girolamo Fracostoro showed that diseases are often spread from one person to another by infection. Miguel Serveto realized that blood is pumped through the lungs by arteries from the heart. Others found safer ways of treating wounds caused in battle, especially the increasing number from gunfire.

Flying machines

Not all the inventions actually worked. The great artist and engineer Leonardo da Vinci was determined to find a way of making people fly like the birds. His grandest idea was for an aircraft with flapping wings, which he dreamed up in about 1503. He organized a test flight but according to legend the machine crashed.

We know very little about the early history of Africa. There must have been great civilizations there, but very few of them developed writing or left any records.

Distant Empires

Some African civilizations built fine communities, such as the east coast port of Kilwa or the mysterious stone complex of Great Zimbabwe. After about AD 700, Muslims from the Near East began to take over many coastal regions and trade routes.

Indian city of Delhi founded by Turks.	c.1206
Foundation of Muslim kingdom of Mali.	1240
Great Zimbabwe built in southern Africa.	c.1270
Mali Empire at its height.	c.1330
Ali of Songhai conquers Timbuktu.	1469
Songhai Empire at its height.	c.1500
Babur begins conquest of northern India.	1526
Akbar conquers Bihar and Bengal for Moghul Empire.	1576

King of Mali

One of the wealthiest of the medieval African empires was Mali. Starting in 1240, its Islamic rulers built up a kingdom stretching for around 990 miles over West Africa. Much of the land was desert, but Mali grew rich from gold. Merchants brought gold there from mines in the south, and traded it for salt and other vital goods from the north.

By 1330 the king of Mali was the most powerful man in West Africa. His name was Mansa Musa, and he had amazed the outside world with a trip to Mecca (the holiest city of Islam). He had arrived there with thousands of followers and camel trains carrying gold and other gifts. Mali itself had gold coinage and city streets lined with copper statues.

The Songhai Empire

Later, an even bigger state ruled much of West Africa. In 1500 the Songhai Empire covered an area from the Atlantic coast across to the center of modern Nigeria. The people of the empire started as simple farmers or fishermen, but swiftly took control of the trade routes

▷ The great inland empires of Africa, which were at their most influential between about 1100 and 1550.

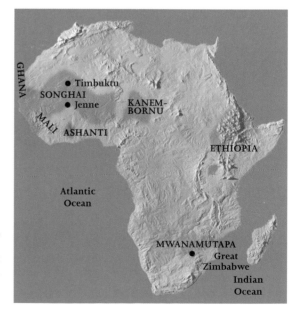

▷ The tomb of Humayan, one of the founders of the Moghul Empire. Humayan was the son of Babur, and father of Akbar. He was ruler of the Empire from 1530–1556.

△ The young Akbar. In later life he was revered by European visitors as "The Great Moghul." He proved himself to be a brave warrior and a wise ruler.

across the Sahara. They exchanged products from Europe and Arabia for gold and other goods from the south. The armies of Muslim Songhai conquered the wealthy cities of Timbuktu and Jenne.

Empire of the Moghuls

Many different peoples had invaded India since the Dark Ages. Huns came from central Asia and Muslim armies from Arabia and Persia. Since 1206 the largest city, Delhi, had been the center of an Islamic state. In 1526 came the greatest conqueror so far – Babur, founder of the Moghul Empire.

The first emperor

Babur was born into a warlike family. He was a descendant of not only Genghis Khan but also the terrifying Timur Lang, who had ravaged India a century earlier. Babur invaded Afghanistan, then crossed the Indus and defeated the Sultan of Delhi at the battle of Pannipat. This gave him firm control over much of northern India.

Akbar, Babur's grandson, came to the throne in 1556, and reigned for nearly 50 years. He extended his dynasty's rule over much of India, uniting most of the north and conquering parts of the south.

Great Zimbabwe

A view showing what the Great Enclosure inside the city of Great Zimbabwe may have looked like. The buildings were made of stone, which is unusual. At that time most structures in Africa would have been built from clay.

△ A figurine of an African chieftain. The civilizations of West Africa had a long artistic tradition of producing fine metalwork.

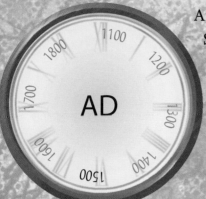

AD

After Columbus's expedition of 1492, many Spaniards volunteered to sail out to the West Indies and South America. They thought they would make their fortunes from the gold and other treasures which lay waiting to be plundered.

The Conquest of the New World

1519	Cortez lands on Mexican coast.
1521	Cortez storms Tenochtitlan and defeats Aztecs.
1532	Pizarro conquers Inca Empire of Peru.
1539	De Soto lands on Florida coast.
1540	Spanish begin convoy system for safe transport of treasure across the Atlantic.
1542	Orellana completes first expedition across South America, down the Amazon.
1549	Huge find of silver at Potosi in Peru.
1561	Aguirre leads first expedition across the Amazon Basin.

At first the hopes of the Spanish adventurers were dashed. The Indians of the Caribbean islands and the American coast had little gold. They could not even be sold as slaves, because most of them died quickly of European diseases caught from the settlers.

Expedition inland

In 1519, a force of 650 Spanish troops sailed from Cuba to explore the Mexican interior. Led by Hernando Cortez, the expedition sailed to the Gulf coast and marched inland. They were now in the land of the Aztecs, a century-old empire extending from the Pacific to the Atlantic. The capital city was Tenochtitlan, with a population of over 100,000 – more than any Spanish city at that time.

The Aztec emperor, Montezuma, sent messengers to meet Cortez with gifts and to warn the Spaniards to turn back. But Cortez marched on, right into the middle of Tenochtitlan, and took the emperor hostage.

The end of the Aztecs

Montezuma had a huge and well-trained army, many times bigger than

△ The Spanish troops were hugely outnumbered when fighting the well-trained army of the Aztec emperor Montezuma. However, the invaders had the advantage of horses, metal armor and guns. Also, many Aztecs believed that the Spaniards were actually gods.

△ *In search of gold and silver, Francisco Pizarro went into Peru with a party of only 180 men – far smaller even than the force led by Cortez. The Spaniards' steel weapons and horses terrified the native peoples.*

Treasure fleets

By 1550, Spain ruled most of Central and South America and the West Indies. Fleets of Spanish galleons carried gold and silver and plundered treasures across the Atlantic to Europe.

the Spanish force, but his enemies had more powerful weapons. The Spaniards were able to seize the palace and kill Montezuma. Cortez then managed to escape from the angry mob in Tenochtitlan. He gathered fresh troops and destroyed the city, forcing the Aztecs to surrender in 1521. He now controlled all Mexico, seizing its treasures and turning the Aztecs into slaves.

Pizarro in Peru

Soon, news reached the Spaniards in Central America of a much wealthier empire in the south. This belonged to the Incas of Peru. In 1532, Francisco Pizarro advanced into Peru with a small party of men. Pizarro copied one of the tactics used by Cortez. He swiftly kidnapped the Inca ruler Atahualpa, and demanded a massive ransom in return for his release. When the ransom was paid, Pizarro had Atahualpa murdered.

Pizarro went on to capture the capital, Cuzco, and the whole Inca Empire collapsed. Within a few years the Spanish conquerors, or "conquistadors," had overrun Peru, Bolivia, and Chile. For well over a century, Spanish treasure ships filled with gold and jewels taken from conquered peoples and silver from the rich mines at Potosi were carried back across the Atlantic to Spain, making it the richest country in Europe.

" These great buildings rising from the water, all made of stone, seemed like a city made by a sorcerer.
ACCOUNT BY A SPANIARD ON FIRST SEEING THE CITY OF TENOCHTITLAN "

△ *A steel helmet worn by the Spanish conquerors. It was held on by a leather strap beneath the chin. The thick metal ridge on top gave solid protection against hefty blows.*

Martin Luther was a Catholic monk from Germany. In 1510 he visited Rome, the home of the Catholic church, and was deeply shocked. He saw the Pope and his household living in great luxury, surrounded by costly paintings, sculpture, and music.

The Reformation

The Catholic church was bloated with wealth and power. Many of its priests were corrupt or just ignorant (some could not even read), and Luther believed that Christ's original teachings had been discarded.

Luther's revolution

In 1517, Luther went to Wittenberg Castle church and nailed a piece of paper to the door. On it was a list of 95 arguments against the sale of "indulgences" by priests – which promised pardon for sins in exchange for cash. Luther went on to attack other abuses of the Christian religion and stated that God judged people by the strength of their faith, not by how much money they gave to the church.

He begged the nobles of Germany to help him reform the old

Luther nails his 95 theses at Wittenberg, Germany.	1517
Pope excommunicates Luther from the Roman Catholic church.	1520–1521
Protestant princes in Germany form the Schmalkaldic League.	1531
Henry VIII becomes head of the Church of England.	1534
King Christian makes Lutheranism the state religion of Denmark.	1536
Pope approves the Society of Jesuits to spearhead a "counter-Reformation."	1540
Calvin publishes his revolutionary ideas for church government.	1541
St. Bartholomew's Day massacre of Huguenots in France.	1572

△ Luther nailed his list of 95 arguments against the church's sale of indulgences to the door of Wittenberg Castle church in 1517. His ideas quickly spread across northern Europe.

△ King Henry VIII of England defied the Pope and declared himself head of the church. In 1532, he introduced laws to cut off England from Rome's power.

△ During the Reformation, the Bible became available for all to read, thanks to the new printing technology. Also, for the first time it was translated from Latin into local languages.

Monasteries

The ruins of Tintern Abbey in Wales. In 1536, Henry VIII ordered that monasteries such as Tintern be "dissolved," or closed down and ransacked.

religion. This alarmed the Pope, who sent an order, or "Bull," that declared Luther was a heretic and that ousted him from the church. Luther burned the Bull in public. He was now an outlaw.

Birth of Protestantism

A number of German princes met at Speyer in 1529, and protested against the Pope's treatment of Luther. From then, the movement became known as Protestantism. Catholics and Protestants formed rival leagues, thus splitting the Christian world in two. Meanwhile, the demand for religious reform was growing fast. Luther's ideas spread to the countries of Scandinavia by the early 1530s. In Switzerland, Huldreich Zwingli and John Calvin established their own new forms of the Protestant religion.

Reforming the church

Very soon Europe was divided in two. On one side were the strongly Catholic countries such as France, Spain, and the Italian states. On the other were newly Protestant countries such as England, Denmark, and the German states. In spite of this crisis, the Pope at first ignored all calls for reform.

The Reformation caused strains in Europe which quickly led to persecution and war. On a single day in 1572, more than 3,000 Huguenots (French Protestants) were massacred by mobs all over France. Catholic monarchs tried to force Protestant countries to return to the old faith and launched themselves into long wars. Philip II of Spain spent many years attempting to invade England and defeat the Protestant queen, Elizabeth I.

◁ A heretic is led to the stake to be burned to death. Many hundreds died in this way. They were not all Protestants, but had often been condemned for disagreeing with the Catholic church's teachings.

AD

"God has not yet ordained that England shall perish." These were the words of Elizabeth I as her country faced invasion by Spain in 1588. But she could have said them many times during her long reign.

The Age of Elizabeth

Elizabeth born in London, second daughter of Henry VIII.	1533
Elizabeth becomes queen upon the death of her sister Mary.	1558
Laws passed to establish the Protestant faith in England.	1559
Mary Queen of Scots takes refuge in England.	1568
The Pope excommunicates Elizabeth and declares she has no right to rule.	1570
Mary Queen of Scots executed.	1587
The defeat of the Spanish Armada.	1588
The Nine Years' War begins in Ireland against English rule.	1594
Death of Elizabeth and end of the Tudor dynasty.	1603

When she had been crowned queen 30 years earlier, both Elizabeth and her throne were in great danger. The previous queen, her sister Mary, had tried to turn England back into a Catholic country again, causing rebellion and bloodshed.

Many powerful people did not believe that an even younger, and still unmarried woman was strong enough to rule any better.

A Protestant monarch

Elizabeth soon showed herself to be tough and decisive and chose intelligent advisers. In 1559 she pushed through laws which confirmed England as a Protestant nation, with priests ordered to use the new English Prayer Book. In 1572 she made an alliance with France to give England support against her many Catholic enemies.

Wisely, the queen refused to get married. Many kings and princes – both Catholic and Protestant – wooed her, but she stayed single. She knew that a foreign husband would make her unpopular with her subjects.

△ One of the most devastating weapons used against the Spanish were fireships, burning boats sent in among the fleet. Attacked by warships and scattered by a terrible storm, the Spanish Armada could only escape by heading to the north of Scotland. Only 60 ships reached home.

△ Elizabeth ended her reign as one of the best-loved and most successful of all English rulers. Her country was stronger and more peaceful than it had ever been.

Mary, Queen of Scots

Mary was not a good ruler. In 1568 she was forced to flee Scotland and find refuge in England. Here she soon became the center of many Catholic plots to overthrow her cousin Elizabeth, who kept her a prisoner.

Mary, Queen of Scots

Catholic leaders of Europe, especially Philip II of Spain, were eager to get rid of the Protestant Elizabeth. But who would take her throne? The ideal replacement was Elizabeth's cousin Mary Stuart. Mary was already a queen (of Scotland), and she was a Catholic. Better still, she had a son and heir, and Elizabeth had none. By 1587, Mary had become too big a threat to Elizabeth. She was tried for treason, found guilty, and beheaded.

The Spanish Armada

Philip of Spain had once hoped to return England to Catholicism by marrying Queen Elizabeth. She had refused him. Now, he decided to change England's religion by force. The execution of Mary Stuart gave him the perfect excuse. In 1588, Philip assembled a fleet of 130 ships and sent them to pick up soldiers from the Netherlands and invade England. The great Spanish "Armada" sailed across the English Channel, but never reached its goal.

The defeat of the Armada did not end the war with Spain – it dragged on for another 16 years, but there were no more big battles. Elizabeth also faced unrest in Ireland, which was still largely Catholic. Her armies could not defeat the rebels, who had to be starved into surrender.

△ Elizabeth's signature on the death warrant of Mary Stuart. Elizabeth hesitated for days before signing it. She knew Mary's death would give her Catholic enemies an excuse to attack her.

"I know I have the body of a weak and feeble woman, but I have the heart and stomach of a king, and of a king of England too.

QUEEN ELIZABETH I, (1533–1603)"

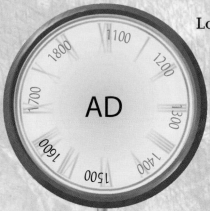

AD

London in about 1600 was dirty, plague-ridden, and overcrowded. Many people were poor and worked very hard and long hours, yet they still enjoyed themselves. They drank in the city's many public houses or watched cruel sports.

Plays and Poets

William Shakespeare born in Stratford-upon-Avon, Warwickshire.	1564
The Red Lion, London's first modern theater, is opened.	1567
Byrd and Tallis publish a collection of choral settings.	1575
Hilliard paints his series of miniatures.	1580–1600
Shakespeare probably writes his earliest plays.	1589
Edmund Spenser begins his long poem, The Faerie Queene.	1590
First performance of Shakespeare's Hamlet.	1601
Death of William Shakespeare.	1616

Best of all, Londoners liked to go to the playhouses. Here, after paying a penny, they could see a marvelous world, full of color and romance, with heroes, clowns, lovers, witches, and even pitched battles on the stage. More than 15,000 people flocked to see such plays every week.

The players

Being an actor was not very glamorous in early Elizabethan times. "Players" were thought to be tramps and troublemakers, who made their living by putting on plays in marketplaces, village greens, and inn yards. After a performance, they would pass around a hat for spectators to throw money in.

In 1572, a new law forced the players to organize themselves better. They had to have a patron, who supported them, and they had to pay for a special license. After this, several bands, or companies, of players built their own permanent theaters, where the audiences had to pay to enter.

William Shakespeare

One of the most famous of these companies was called The Lord Chamberlain's Men. Their success was largely due to the man who wrote many of their plays – William Shakespeare. He developed a new kind of verse drama, ranging from

▷ London's Globe Theatre. In Shakespeare's time, ordinary spectators watched from the ground where there were no seats. A seat in the covered galleries was more expensive.

22

▷ Many musical instruments in the Middle Ages were forerunners of those played today. The big fiddle became the modern violin. The shawm (far left) was an early version of the recorder.

comedies such as *Much Ado About Nothing* to bloody tragedies such as *Macbeth*. These explored the whole range of human feelings in language that any Elizabethan could easily understand. These emotions – love, hatred, jealousy, and ambition – make Shakespeare's plays as relevant and interesting today as they were 400 years ago.

The Globe Theatre

The Chamberlain's Men performed at the Globe, on the bank of the River Thames. Shakespeare described it as "this wooden O," and it was shaped as a hollow circle with a stage at one side. An Elizabethan playhouse was a noisy place. Actors had to make themselves heard above the talking, eating, and drinking of the audience, who would shout at the actors if they didn't like them.

Poets and painters

The period around 1600 saw a flowering of many other arts in Britain. Edmund Spenser wrote his epic poem in praise of Elizabeth I, *The Faerie Queene*. Among leading artists was Nicholas Hilliard, who painted delicate miniature portraits. Composers such as William Byrd and Thomas Tallis created rich choral music.

△ William Shakespeare was the greatest poet and playwright of the Elizabethan age. Before him, very few good plays had ever been written in the English language.

Don Quixote

An illustration from *Don Quixote*, a novel in two parts (1605 and 1615) by the Spanish writer Miguel de Cervantes. It tells the story of a landowner who, attracted by tales of knights of old, dresses up in armor and sets out to perform heroic deeds. The down-to-earth attitude of his trusty servant Sancho Panzo contrasts with Quixote's own idealism.

△ An inkwell and quill pen. The feather was trimmed before it was used, and the point sharpened with a knife was also used to scrape out mistakes.

AD

"There never has been and never will be a more dreadful happening," wrote a monk after the Turks captured Constantinople in 1453. But he was wrong. The Christian world was going to get many more shocks from the Ottoman invaders during the next 200 years.

Suleiman the Magnificent

Suleiman "the Magnificent" becomes Ottoman sultan.	1520
Hungarian king defeated at battle of Mohacz.	1526
Death of Suleiman.	1566
Turkish fleet defeated at battle of Lepanto.	1571
Sinan completes building of his masterpiece, the Selimye Mosque at Edirne.	1574
Turks regain Baghdad after losing it to the Persians.	1638
Turks join with Cossacks to invade Poland.	1672
The siege of Vienna. Turkish army routed by allied troops.	1683

Constantinople became the new center of the Ottoman empire, which continued to grow until it included large parts of southeastern Europe. The Ottomans seized Muslim lands too, conquering Syria in 1516 and Egypt a year later, taking control of the three holy cities of Islam – Medina, Mecca, and Jerusalem.

The Great Sultan

In 1520 the greatest of the Ottoman rulers came to the throne. His name was Suleiman, and he was soon to become known as "The Magnificent" because of the splendor of his court and the might of his armies. His capital Constantinople, renamed Istanbul, was the biggest city in the world.

Suleiman set out to expand his empire still farther. He captured cities as far apart as Belgrade, Baghdad, and Algiers, as well as Aden and the island of Rhodes. In 1526 he smashed the forces of the Hungarian king at the battle of Mohacz. Meanwhile his navy, led by the corsair Barbarossa, ruled the Mediterranean.

Patron and law-giver

Suleiman was not just a fine leader and warrior. He was also a poet and a scholar.

△ After the death of Suleiman the Turks continued to be victorious in battle, capturing the Christian island of Cyprus in 1571. But in the same year came a defeat at Lepanto (above) off the Greek coast, when 200 Turkish warships were sunk or captured by the Spanish and Italian fleets.

△ Suleiman I was a wise and noble emperor, but he quarreled with his sons and had two of them executed.

Islamic art

The empire brought Suleiman great wealth, which he used to hire the best artists and architects. Among them was Mirman Sinan, who designed at least 165 mosques and palaces.

Suleiman was also known as *al-Qanuni*, "the law-giver." He had complete control over the daily lives of his subjects and chose slaves from his own bodyguard to govern the provinces of the empire. He also reformed the legal system, so that land rents and taxes were collected properly.

Defeat at Lepanto

After Suleiman's death in 1566, the Ottoman Empire continued to grow. But the defeat at the battle of Lepanto in 1571 marked a long and slow decline in the Ottomans' power. Their later leaders were often weak or mad – Mehmed III had all 19 of his brothers put to death in 1595 so he would have no rivals! The huge empire had become difficult to govern, and there were mutinies in the army.

The final advance

Yet the Turks were still the greatest power in Europe and Asia. They even began a new program of conquest, invading Poland in 1672 and Austria in 1683. But this was as far as they got. The Ottoman army laid siege to the Austrian capital, Vienna, but could not capture it. After three months, they were attacked by an allied force and driven away. The once dreaded Turks were never a threat to Europe again.

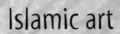

I who am Sultan of Sultans, the sovereign of sovereigns, ... the shadow of God on earth, the Sultan lord of the White Sea and of the Black Sea ...
EXTRACT FROM LETTER WRITTEN BY SULEIMAN

△ Intricate detail from a Persian carpet shows birds, animals, and trees. Such subjects were rare, for the Islamic religion in the Middle East banned images of living things.

During the 1600s and 1700s, Western Europe became the center of world power. The strong nations, such as Britain, Spain, and France, took control of countries far overseas. They used trade to open up worldwide links.

Empires and Industry

These powerful European countries established bases on the African coast, in Southeast Asia, India, Australia, and South, Central, and North America. Some of these bases grew into colonies, and the collections of colonies gradually began to develop into large-scale empires.

Revolution in industry

These empires brought vast amounts of goods into Europe. At the same time, they were markets where European goods could be sold. This revolution in trade was part of another revolution – in industry. The newly discovered power of coal and steam, and the invention of new machines, helped to produce more iron that cost less, cotton cloth, and other valuable products. Factories started to replace cottage workshops, and peasants moved to the expanding cities to find work. Farmers developed ways of growing more food to feed the rapidly increasing populations of the cities and towns.

Strong leaders

This was also an age of mighty monarchs. Leaders such as Peter the Great of Russia and Frederick the Great of Prussia almost single-handedly turned disunited and backward countries into major world powers. Most glittering of all was Louis XIV of France, who became known as the "Sun King." Other kings failed miserably. The weaknesses of Charles I drove England to a bitter civil war and ended with his own execution.

Europe at war

In fact, the countries of Europe spent most of their time fighting each other during this period. In all of the 1600s, there were only four years of complete peace. Armies and navies grew bigger and more heavily armed, and battles in the 1700s sometimes involved hundreds of thousands of troops. But European armies did not always win. In 1783, Britain was forced to admit defeat and give freedom to her North American colonies. The United States of America was born.

The Spanish were the first Europeans to land large numbers of people on the American continent. They were also the first to conquer territory, seizing the empires of the Aztecs in Mexico and the Inca peoples in Peru.

New World Colonies

By about 1600 Spanish and Portuguese explorers had taken control of much of South and Central America. The huge expanse of North America still lay open and unknown. It contained no gold and silver, but there were vast resources of timber and valuable furs, and fertile land for growing crops.

Spanish found city of St. Augustine, in Florida.	1565
First English attempt at settlement, on Roanoke Island.	1585
James I grants charter to establish colonies in Virginia.	1606
French build a fort at the site of Quebec.	1608
The Pilgrims found Plymouth Colony in New England.	1620
Dutch establish their first settlement at Manhattan, called New Netherland.	1624
First settlers in Massachusetts.	1633
The population of Virginia reaches 5,000.	1643

The first colonies

Spain and France got an early foothold in the north. The French explorer Jacques Cartier reached the Gulf of the St. Lawrence River in 1534, and traveled to the site of modern Montreal. To the south, a small French colony was set up in Florida. Spanish settlers destroyed this in 1565 and created their own. The Spanish city of St. Augustine is the oldest in North America.

The English soon followed. In 1583 Humphrey Gilbert claimed Newfoundland in the name of Elizabeth I. In 1585 Walter Raleigh placed settlers on the island of Roanoke, off the Carolina coast. This was the first English settlement, but it only lasted for a year.

Virginia and Quebec

It was not until 1607 that about 100 English settlers landed on the

△ Many settlers lived along the New England coast, where there were plentiful supplies of timber to build their homes and to build ships. The early settlers built houses which were similar to those back in England, with thatched roofs and stone chimneys.

△ This painting by the American artist George H. Boughton shows a group of Pilgrims walking to church. The men are armed with muskets to protect the group from attack by local native peoples.

The Mayflower

A modern replica of the *Mayflower*, the ship in which the first Pilgrims set sail from England in 1620. They founded the Plymouth Colony in what is now Massachusetts.

American east coast and founded a sizeable colony. They called it Virginia (in honor of Elizabeth I, "The Virgin Queen"), and named the first city Jamestown (in honor of James I). Soon after, the explorer Champlain built a small fort at Quebec on the St. Lawrence River. This was the first French settlement in what became Canada.

Hard times

At first, life was a bitter struggle for the pioneer settlers. Crops failed, winters were harsh and there were disputes with the native peoples. Food was so scarce in Quebec that fresh supplies had to be brought from France.

Things got better slowly. The settlers began to grow a new and valuable crop for exporting to Europe – tobacco. They made treaties with the friendly local Indians, and supplied them with firearms to help defeat their enemies.

In 1620, a shipload of Puritans from England set up a second colony in New England. They are known as the Pilgrims. From here, they spread out to establish New Hampshire in 1623 and Connecticut in 1633.

△ In the colonies, girls would embroider samplers – squares of cloth decorated with words and patterns of needlework. They usually added their name and age, as well as the date.

> They may beginne their first plantation and seat of their first habitation at any place on the coaste of Virginia.
>
> ## EXTRACT FROM CHARTER GRANTED BY JAMES I
>
> *King James I of England granted a charter which allowed people from England to settle in the New World.*

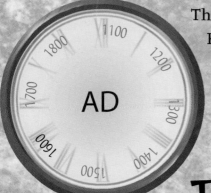

AD

The bloody struggle between Catholics and Protestants in Europe lasted for more than a century. It was made up of a series of great "wars of religion," which involved countries as far apart as the Netherlands, Spain, Sweden, France, and England.

The Thirty Years' War

The last and biggest of these religious wars began where the Reformation itself had begun – in the bickering states of Germany. This messy conflict became known as the Thirty Years' War.

The "defenestration" of Catholic officials in Prague.	1618
Bohemian Protestants defeated by Spain at White Mountain.	1620
Danish army invades northern Germany.	1625
Gustavus Adolphus of Sweden defeats Spanish at Breitenfeld.	1631
Swedish army destroyed at Nordlingen.	1634
France declares war on Habsburg Spain.	1635
French and Swedes invade Bavaria.	1646
Treaty of Westphalia ends the war in Germany.	1648

Out of the window
The war started in a dramatic way. Protestants in Bohemia (now part of the Czech Republic) were angry with their new king, Ferdinand. He was a member of the powerful Spanish Habsburg family and wanted to restore Bohemia to the Catholic faith. He closed Protestant schools and in 1618 ordered that Protestant churches in Prague be pulled down.

The Protestants banded together and threw some Catholic officials from an upstairs window in Prague Castle. The incident sparked off a civil war in Bohemia. In 1619 the rebels expelled Ferdinand and chose a new king, the Protestant Frederick.

The war spreads
Two days later, Ferdinand became the new Holy Roman

△ In 1618 Protestants invaded the royal palace in Prague. They seized a number of Catholic officials and threw them out of an upstairs window. This event became known as the "Defenestration of Prague."

▷ The French army, under its leader Louis II, Prince of Condé, was victorious at the battle of Rocroi in 1643. The French troops destroyed the best of the Spanish infantry.

△ During the 1600s the magnificent Palace of Versailles was built outside Paris. It was the residence of the French royal family. The palace contains paintings and sculptures by artists from all over Europe.

emperor, with massive new powers. He immediately used these to take revenge on the Bohemians, defeating them at White Mountain in 1620. Frederick fled, and Catholicism was the state religion again.

Ferdinand's army pushed on into northern Germany, alarming other Protestant countries. Christian IV of Denmark organized a Protestant army and invaded Germany in 1625, but the Catholic forces were too strong and defeated him.

The turning point

The next to enter the war was King Gustavus Adolphus of Sweden, determined to protect his small country against Ferdinand. A small, well-trained army defeated the Spanish at Breitenfeld in 1631. A year later the Swedes won a second great victory at Lutzen. The Swedish army was eventually defeated in 1634. But now help came from a surprising ally – Catholic France. The French supported the Protestants because Cardinal Richelieu, France's most powerful man, wanted to stop the growth of Spanish control in Europe.

Richelieu declared war on Spain in 1635, attacking its territories in Spain and Italy. By 1648 the war was over. Spain's power in Europe was broken, and three decades of war left Germany in ruins.

Rembrandt

The master Dutch painter Rembrandt van Rijn was at work during the period of the Thirty Years' War. He produced a great number of works of art, including around 600 paintings and 100 or so self-portraits, such as the one seen here. By the late 1630s Rembrandt was Amsterdam's most fashionable portrait artist.

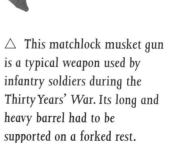

△ This matchlock musket gun is a typical weapon used by infantry soldiers during the Thirty Years' War. Its long and heavy barrel had to be supported on a forked rest.

AD

In 1603, Britain had a new monarch – James I. He was the first of the Stuart kings, and ruled not only England and Wales, but also Scotland. James believed strongly that God had given kings their right to govern, and no one could question this authority.

Civil Wars in Britain

James' arrogant views and behavior made him very unpopular with his subjects. His son Charles I, who followed him to the throne in 1625, was even less popular. Soon Britain was split by civil wars.

Trouble with parliament

Charles wanted to rule without consulting parliament. In 1629 he dismissed parliament, and did not call another for 11 years. But he needed to raise taxes to pay for a bigger army – and he had to have parliament's agreement for this.

By 1640 Charles was facing rebellion. The Scots had invaded northern England, and the English army was weak and ill-equipped. Reluctantly, Charles summoned parliament and asked for permission to raise new taxes. A rebellion in Ireland in 1641 meant that Charles now needed an even bigger army, but members of parliament demanded that the king hand over the army command to them.

Charles I becomes king.	1625
English defeated by Scots in first "Bishops' War."	1639
Catholic rebellion in Ireland.	1641
Charles declares war on parliament.	1642
Roundhead victory at Marston Moor.	1644
New Model Army created. Royalist army smashed at Naseby.	1645
"Second" civil war.	1648
Execution of Charles I.	1649
Cromwell becomes Lord Protector.	1653
Restoration of the monarchy.	1660

△ *A combined force of Scots and Roundheads defeated Charles and his Royalist forces at the battle of Marston Moor, in Yorkshire, in 1644.*

▷ Charles I was brought to trial by the English parliament. He was found guilty of treason against his own subjects and beheaded outside Whitehall Palace, London on January 31, 1649.

△ A Roundhead (left) and a Royalist soldier (right). Roundheads wore iron helmets and breastplates for protection.

War begins

Enraged by this, Charles tried to arrest five members of parliament for treason. The action made him hated all the more, and he was forced to flee London. By August 1642 he had declared war on the parliamentary supporters (known as "Roundheads"). He tried to retake London but his Royalists were beaten back at Turnham Green.

Defeat and execution

By 1644 the parliamentary side had the advantage, having gained a powerful ally in the Scots. To make sure of victory, they needed one more decisive battle. Inspired by Oliver Cromwell, the Roundheads crushed the Royalists at Naseby in 1645 and captured the king.

The Restoration

After the execution of Charles I in 1649, England had no King for the next 11 years (England became a Commonwealth). The new leader was Oliver Cromwell, who was appointed Lord Protector until his death in 1658. Two years later, Charles II (son of Charles I) was invited back from exile and crowned king. This event was known as the Restoration.

Oliver Cromwell

After the execution of Charles I, Cromwell was made Lord Protector. He had been a very successful commander during the Civil War, and was a strong leader. However, he did not get along well with parliament. His son, Richard, took over as Lord Protector after Cromwell's death in 1658, but was forced to abdicate soon after, when Charles II, son of Charles I, was made king.

△ A Roundhead helmet. Oliver Cromwell reorganized the Roundhead forces into a professional force known as the "New Model Army."

"If I have seen further," wrote Isaac Newton, "it is by standing on the shoulders of giants." Newton was the greatest scientist of his age, but he knew that his success was built on the work of great thinkers and researchers before him.

The New Science

The 1600s was a golden age for science, with astonishing advances in many areas from astronomy to medicine, and from biology to mathematics.

Student genius

In 1665, following a new outbreak of plague, universities were closed and the students sent home. Young Isaac Newton of Cambridge University used his long holiday to work out the ideas which were buzzing around in his head. First, he uncovered the secrets of light and color. He passed a beam of sunlight through an angled glass "prism." This split the white light into a rainbow band of colors. When he passed the rainbow through a second prism, it was mixed back into white light again. Next, Newton watched the way an apple fell to the

1657 — Huygens invents the first clock to be driven by a pendulum.

1666 — Newton discovers the nature of white light by passing it through a prism.

1668 — Newton builds his first reflecting (mirror) telescope.

c. 1670 — Japanese mathematician Seki Kowa solves simultaneous equations.

c. 1680 — Malpighi confirms Harvey's theory about the circulation of the blood.

1683 — Van Leeuwenhoek invents the precision microscope.

1687 — Newton publishes his Mathematical Principles.

1714 — Fahrenheit invents the mercury thermometer.

△ Isaac Newton at work in his study. Later, he expanded his theories about gravity to show how it is linked with movement.

△ The English scientist Robert Hooke used an early microscope such as this one to discover the existence of living cells in plants.

Harvey's circulation

William Harvey discovered how blood circulates through vessels in the bodies of humans. This is his diagram of the veins in the human arm.

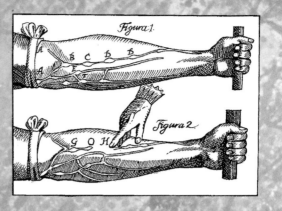

ground. He realized that objects were pulled toward the earth by a force he named gravity.

Looking at the heavens

Newton became the first person to use a telescope to see the moons orbiting the planet Jupiter. He also used his theories about gravity to show why the planets orbit the sun. Edmond Halley was greatly influenced by his friend Newton's work. In 1676 he made a catalog of the stars which can be seen from the southern half of the world. He also studied the way objects such as comets move.

△ Edmond Halley correctly predicted that a comet which he had seen in 1683 would reappear in 1759. (This is now known as Halley's Comet, and it last appeared in 1986.)

Microscopes and medicine

Other scientists were looking inward at the secrets of the human body. They were able to use a new instrument to help them – the two-lens microscope which had been invented in about 1590. During the 1670s, Italian physician Marcello Malpighi made a close study of the lungs, liver, and other organs. Dutchman Antonie van Leeuwenhoek made the most powerful microscope of the time, which could make objects appear up to 270 times bigger. He was the first to identify red corpuscles in blood.

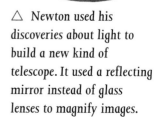

△ Newton used his discoveries about light to build a new kind of telescope. It used a reflecting mirror instead of glass lenses to magnify images.

"I seem to have been only like a boy playing on the sea-shore . . . whilst the great ocean of truth lay all undiscovered before me.
SIR ISAAC NEWTON (1642–1727)

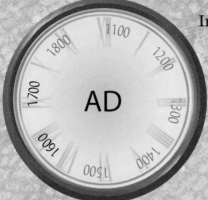

AD

In many ways, the stories of China and Japan in the 1600s look very similar. Both were united and peaceful under a strong military rule. Both were growing wealthier and more thickly populated.

China and Japan

China was the world's richest and most powerful country in the 1600s. It had a population of about 150 million – almost twice as big as that of Europe. Production of food in China (especially the country's all-important rice crop) rose rapidly during this period.

Triumph of the Ching

The Manchu people had invaded China from the northeast, completing their conquest in 1644. They placed on the throne a new dynasty, or family, of emperors called the Ching. Although the Manchu people were foreigners, they soon adopted traditional Chinese customs and culture.

The greatest of the early Ching emperors was K'ang-hsi, whose long reign lasted until 1722. His armies extended the Chinese Empire to include Taiwan, Tibet, Turkestan, and Outer Mongolia. K'ang-hsi was not just a clever general, he was also a wise and tolerant ruler. He encouraged foreign traders and Catholic scholars to visit China, and he traveled widely to see his subjects.

A declining empire

However, this prosperity could not last. During the 1700s, China's population grew at an even faster rate, reaching about 320 million by 1800. It was impossible to grow enough rice, and

Tokugawa clan takes control of Japan.	1603
All foreign traders banned from Japanese soil apart from the Dutch.	1641
Manchus conquer China, ending the Ming dynasty.	1644
Ching dynasty force all Chinese to wear a pigtail.	1645
K'ang-hsi founds porcelain factories in China.	1680
Manchus conquer Taiwan.	1683
Teaching of Christianity banned in China.	1716
Chinese troops invade Tibet.	1751

▷ *A Japanese shogun. The shoguns disliked the influence of foreigners. They wanted to keep Japanese society as it had always been.*

▷ *A Dutch trading ship outside the port of Nagasaki. By 1641 only the Dutch were allowed to trade in Japanese ports, sending one ship each year to Nagasaki.*

△ *Dutch traders tend their allotment while confined by the shoguns to the island of Deshima in Nagasaki Bay.*

there were many food shortages. This led to riots and a full-scale rebellion in 1795, greatly weakening the power of the Ching.

Land of the shoguns

Japan was going along a very different path than China, slowly cutting itself off from the outside world. In 1603, clan leader Tokugawa Ieyasu at last defeated his rivals and established himself as shogun (military ruler) of the whole country. Law and order were enforced by the fierce warrior class called samurai.

Trade was booming by this time. Japan's most precious asset was silver, most of which went to China to pay for raw silk. This was turned into beautiful fabrics and garments and sold to foreign merchants. Spanish, Portuguese, Dutch, and British ships came to trade, bringing firearms and other goods in exchange for the silk.

Expelling the foreigners

The shoguns distrusted the Europeans, especially the Christian missionaries. During the 1630s, they expelled the Spanish and Portuguese traders and began to torture and execute the missionaries and their converts.

▷ *A samurai sword. Following a ban on the use of guns, the only legal weapons were swords, bows and arrows, and spears. Only the samurai were allowed to carry them.*

The tea trade

Dutch traders shipped tea from China to Europe for the first time in 1610. Tea drinking soon became popular, particularly in Britain. European ships queued outside China's ports to load up with tea and other goods. This engraving shows tea traders buying and selling tea for export.

AD

Peter the Great was a giant figure, well over six feet tall, and full of violent energy. When he became tsar (emperor) of Russia in 1696, he was determined to use all his energy to make Russia a strong and modern state.

The Rise of Russia

After many years of civil war, invasion, and bloodshed, Russia had just begun a slow progress out of its backward and primitive past. Under the new tsar, this progress became far more rapid.

Learning from Europe

Peter spent two years touring western Europe to find out for himself how other countries were run. He visited England, Austria, Holland, and Germany, looking at factories, mills, and science laboratories. He even worked in a London shipyard and learned how to be a dentist! Back home in Russia, Peter put what he had learned into practice. He set up new high schools and urged the children of nobles to study abroad.

City in the swamp

Peter was also a great builder. He built new roads and canals, and introduced modern methods to mining and other industries. He ordered the building of a complete new capital city on marshy land near the Baltic coast. The city of St. Petersburg became one of the most beautiful cities in the world.

For decades, the Russian army had been weak and ill-equipped. Peter turned it into a modern force, with new weapons, able officers, and

At the age of nine, Peter becomes joint ruler with his brother.	1682
Peter becomes sole tsar of all Russia.	1696
Peter makes grand tour of western Europe.	1696–1698
Founding of new city of St. Petersburg.	1703
Major victory over Swedes at battle of Poltava.	1705
Death of Peter the Great.	1725
Murder of Peter III; Catherine becomes empress.	1762
Major rebellion of serfs and Cossacks is brutally put down.	1775
Death of Catherine the Great.	1796

△ Russian peasants had a harsh life. Even after Peter's reforms, they still used wooden plows and harrows, instead of iron ones and lived in huts made of timber and mud.

△ Peter the Great started the first Russian newspaper and opened the country's first museums. He reformed the system of government and brought the church under the state's control.

St. Petersburg

The beautiful city of St. Petersburg lies beside the river Neva. Its magnificent Winter Palace was the winter home of the tsars. As a result of working in the difficult marshy conditions, thousands of peasants died while building Peter the Great's new city.

rigorous training. He also used his knowledge of shipbuilding to create a powerful new Russian navy.

Rebellion

For the poor peasants, however, little had changed. These "serfs." who were virtually slaves, made up the vast majority of the Russian population. They lived and worked on the land, where the harsh conditions had barely altered since the Middle Ages. There were many uprisings by peasants and farmers, but the tsar's troops crushed them with great cruelty. After Peter's death in 1725, rivals fought to take his place. In 1762 the reigning tsar, Peter III, was battered to death with a footstool.

Empress of Russia

Russia's next strong ruler was Catherine the Great, wife of the ill-fated Peter III. She plotted his death and succeeded him to the throne. Catherine built more schools and hospitals and abolished capital punishment (except for treason). She made the serfs' lives harder by forcing more work and military service on them, and by tightening their landlords' control over them.

△ Religious paintings that are considered to be sacred by the church in Russia are known as icons. Peter the Great reduced the church's power considerably, as well as the amount of land it owned.

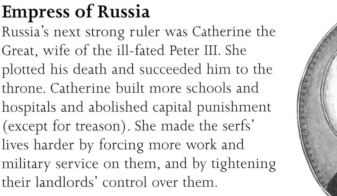

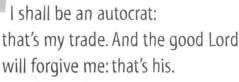

I shall be an autocrat: that's my trade. And the good Lord will forgive me: that's his.
EMPRESS CATHERINE THE GREAT (1729–1796)

In 1700, more than 90 percent of Europe's population lived in the countryside. Most people were peasants working on the land. They grew their own food, using tools and farming methods which had changed very little since medieval times.

The Farming Revolution

At this time Europe's population was about to rise rapidly. By 1800 the number of people in Europe soared from 120 million to over 180 million. Farmers found ways to grow much bigger quantities of crops, and there was enough food to feed many more people.

Enclosing the land

Many villages still used the old system of strip farming, where fields were divided into strips and shared among the farmers for growing crops. Rougher land was left as "common" pasture for grazing. Many animals had to be slaughtered every winter because there was too little feed for them.

One way of improving the quality of food was to enclose the common land with hedges and ditches. This stopped animals from wandering and gave better drainage. It allowed wealthy farmers to buy up land and build bigger, more carefully managed farms. But enclosure also took away common land from poorer people.

Rotating crops

The medieval system of growing crops was wasteful. A field was sown with winter corn one year, spring corn the second, and left fallow, or unplanted, the third year so that it could regain fertility. By about 1650, Dutch farmers had developed a more efficient way of "rotating" their crops.

△ In the four-course crop rotation, wheat was grown in the first year and turnips in the second. Sheep or cattle ate the turnips, providing valuable manure. Barley was sown in the third year, then grass or clover.

Jethro Tull invents the seed drill.	1701
Viscount Townshend develops his system of four-course crop rotation.	1730
Robert Bakewell begins his improved livestock breeding.	1745
New wave of land enclosures in Britain.	1760
Thomas Coke begins program of improving farmland on his estate.	1776
Robert Ransome invents the "self-sharpening" metal plow.	1785
John Deere makes the first all-steel plow.	1837
Fergus McCormick develops his mechanical reaper.	1839

△ Tobacco plants in flower. Farmers in North America began to grow tobacco as a commercial crop in the early 1600s. The first tobacco farms were in Virginia, where the climate and soil were just right.

Tull's seed drill

Since farming began, famers had scattered seed by hand. Jethro Tull's seed drill put the seed directly into the soil in neat rows. This allowed farmers to hoe out weeds between the rows.

Instead of leaving a field fallow, they made it fertile more quickly by spreading manure or growing clover and grasses to improve the soil. In the 1730s, farmers such as Charles Townshend of England began using a four-part system of planting crops in rotation.

Better breeding

The four-course rotation of crops meant that many more animals could be fed through the winter, instead of being killed. Farmers could fatten them up with hay and grain, as well as roots such as swedes and turnips. By keeping them in enclosed fields, the farmers had better control over the animals' health. This opened the way for the animals to be improved by careful breeding. Pioneers such as the Englishman Robert Bakewell did this by selecting the best animals from their herds and breeding them together.

New machines

Scattering seed by hand was wasteful, and a lot of seed was eaten by birds. In about 1701 Jethro Tull invented a machine for sowing seeds more efficiently. In 1785 Robert Ransome devised the first completely cast-iron plow, which stayed sharp.

wheat

"Our farmers round, well pleased with constant gain,
Like other farmers, flourish and complain.
THE PARISH REGISTER, GEORGE CRABBE
(1754–1832)

Crabbe was an English poet who wrote about working class life.

△ As a result of improved breeding techniques, farmers were able to produce sheep which gave better wool. They also had short legs and barrel-like bodies for more meat.

AD

The beginning of the 18th century saw the fading of the old European powers, such as Spain and the Holy Roman Empire. It also saw the end of wars over religion. Instead, three new strong nations were emerging – France, Britain, and Prussia.

War and Rebellion

War of the Spanish succession.	1702–1713
Death of Louis XIV. First Jacobite rebellion in Scotland fails.	1715
Frederick of Prussia invades Silesia.	1740
Second Jacobite rebellion in Scotland suppressed.	1745
Seven Years' War begins.	1756
Robert Clive wins the battle of Plassey in India.	1757
James Wolfe leads British force to capture Quebec.	1759
Seven Years' War ends. Britain gains Canada and all land east of the Mississippi.	1763

United under powerful leaders, the new nations struggled for control of large parts of the continent of Europe. This struggle even spilled over into North America and India and led to several long-running wars.

The Sun King
Louis XIV had come to the throne of France at the age of five in 1643. During his adult life he had built up a strong army and navy and extended French power. He had also inspired a golden age of culture in France.

King Charles II of Spain was just the opposite – weak and sickly. When he died without heirs in 1700 he left his throne to Louis XIV's grandson. Louis grandly declared that France and Spain were united. Alarmed at this, England, Prussia, the Netherlands, and other states formed an alliance against the French. In a long and bitter war, they repeatedly defeated the French. When peace came in 1713, Louis' grandson remained king of Spain, but France and Spain stayed separate.

Great Britain united
The Act of Union in 1707 joined together England, Wales and Scotland. Many Scots hated being ruled from London, and eagerly

△ *At the heart of Louis XIV's reign was a glamorous court, based around his splendid palace at Versailles. Louis chose the sun as his emblem, and was known as the "Sun King."*

△ Bonnie Prince Charlie's proper name was Charles Edward Stuart. The grandson of James II, he was the last member of the Stuart family to try and claim the throne of England.

▷ English troops shattered the Jacobite rebels, led by Bonnie Prince Charlie, at the battle of Culloden in 1746. Prince Charlie had to flee to France. After this, the Act of Union was safe.

supported any attack on the English. James Stuart, the son of James II who had been forced from the English throne in 1688, tried to seize the British crown several times with French support. His followers (called Jacobites) found a more glamorous leader in his son Charles. Bonnie Prince Charlie led the Jacobite army to victory over the English in 1745 but was defeated at the battle of Culloden. the following year.

Frederick the Great

Frederick II of Prussia was a clever and cultured man with interests ranging from music to philosophy. He encouraged agriculture and industry and freed the serfs on the royal estates. His main interest was war and Prussia's growing strength. He invaded Silesia (part of the Austrian Empire) in 1740 and later added parts of Poland.

Angry at Frederick's aggressive tactics, Austria formed an alliance with Russia and France to force him out of Silesia. Frederick invaded Saxony in 1756, marking the start of the Seven Years' War. He then defeated both the French and Austrian armies. In 1758, the British joined Frederick in further battles against their old enemy, France, but Britain's real aim was to extend her empire overseas.

Voltaire

Voltaire was a French philosopher and writer, with a keen sense of justice. He wrote more than 50 plays as well as philosophical stories and poems. As a young man, he was condemned for criticizing the government and spent 11 months in the notorious Bastille prison in Paris.

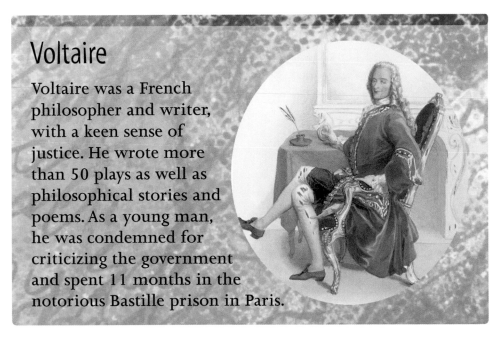

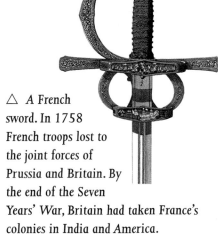

△ A French sword. In 1758 French troops lost to the joint forces of Prussia and Britain. By the end of the Seven Years' War, Britain had taken France's colonies in India and America.

The world was speeding up. During the 1700s, populations began to grow, especially in Europe and North America. These extra people needed more food, more homes and more jobs.

Industrial Revolution

At the same time, industry was expanding at an amazing rate, thanks to the development of new machines, new methods of making things and new sources of power. The result was a dramatic change in the way people lived and worked. We call this change the Industrial Revolution.

Abraham Darby uses coke to smelt iron.	1709
Thomas Newcomen builds the first practical steam pump.	1712
John Kay invents the flying shuttle.	1733
James Hargreaves develops his "spinning jenny."	1764
Improved steam engine built by James Watt.	1769
Eli Whitney invents the cotton gin.	1793
Alessandro Volta assembles the first electric cell.	1800
Friedrich Krupp opens his ironworks in Essen, Germany.	1810
Michael Faraday discovers how to produce an electric current with magnets.	1831

King cotton
The growing demand for cheap cotton cloth transformed the spinning and weaving industry. For centuries, these had been slow processes performed by hand. Now a series of inventions in Britain made them much faster. The "flying shuttle" of the 1730s doubled the speed of weaving. The "spinning jenny" and the "mule" produced spun thread much more quickly and inexpensively. The one big obstacle to the expansion of the cotton industry was removed by Eli Whitney's invention of the cotton gin in 1793. It made the process of cleaning cotton 50 times faster!

Coal and iron
Coal became increasingly important as the fuel for ovens and forges. Coal mines were dug deeper as demand grew, leading to greater dangers of floods, collapse, and gas explosions. Inventions such as Newcomen's

△ The ironworks at Coalbrookdale in Shropshire, England. It was here, in 1709, that ironmaster Abraham Darby discovered that coal could be turned into coke by baking it. With this, he was able to make better quality iron in his furnaces. The iron was needed to make the newly invented industrial machines.

△ Benjamin Franklin was an American statesman as well as a scientist. Franklin proved that lightning and electricity are the same thing by flying a kite in a storm. He was struck by lightning and was lucky to survive.

Cotton Gin

Raw cotton, grown mainly in the United States, was very difficult and slow to clean. Whitney's cotton gin was a simple machine which brushed out the troublesome seeds from the cotton fibers.

steam pump (to remove water) and Davy's safety lamp eased these problems. Abraham Darby's discovery that coal could be turned into coke led to the production of coke-smelted iron. The improved iron could be used to make everything from ploughs and bridges to steam engines and drilling machines.

Steam power

The old sources of power – water, horses, and wind – still drove the new machines. They were soon replaced by a new, less expensive kind of power which never tired – steam. One coal – powered steam engine could do the work of hundreds of horses.

In 1712 Thomas Newcomen devised the first efficient steam pump. James Watt's improved steam engine, built in 1769, could turn wheels. Now steam power could be harnessed to work spinning machines and looms, as well as giant hammers and the bellows for blast furnaces.

Factory life

Machines in factories created millions of new jobs, so many people began to leave the countryside to work in the towns. Houses and factories had to be built for them. By 1850, over 60 percent of Britons lived in towns. Factory workers led hard lives, often working 14 hours a day, six days a week.

"In every cry of every Man/ In every Infant's cry of fear,/ In every voice, in every ban,/ The mind forg'd manacles I hear.

from "LONDON," WILLIAM BLAKE (1757–1827)

Blake wrote several poems about the effects of the Industrial Revolution."

△ Davy's safety lamp warned miners of gas leaks underground. Inventions such as this only encouraged coal miners to go into farther and more dangerous depths.

Britain had started her collection of overseas colonies in the reign of Elizabeth I. By 1602, both England and the Netherlands had founded an "East India Company" on the Indian coast to trade with the Far East.

Britain's Colonies

The first settlements in North America took root and flourished in early Stuart times. In 1661, Britain gained her first African foothold, seizing James Island on the Gambia River. By the middle of the 1700s, these scattered colonies had begun to grow into a powerful and profitable empire.

Ruling the waves

In 1623, Dutch settlers murdered ten English merchants on the island of Amboina in the China Seas. After this, relations grew worse between the two countries. A series of wars began in 1652, only ending in 1868 when the Dutch king, William III, took the British throne.

Over the next 50 years the British navy became bigger and stronger still. With faster and better-armed warships which could sail much closer to the wind, it defeated most other national fleets. By the 1750s British vessels "ruled the waves," making passage easier for merchant ships trading with the developing colonies.

The new colony of Georgia is founded in North America.	1732
Collapse of the Moghul Empire in India.	1739
War breaks out between Britain and France in North America.	1744
Victory at Plassey secures British control of northern India.	1757
French advance south into Ohio.	1753
French surrender Quebec to the British.	1759
Britain gains control of Canada and most land east of the Mississippi.	1763
Abolition of the slave trade in Britain.	1807
George IV crowned King.	1821

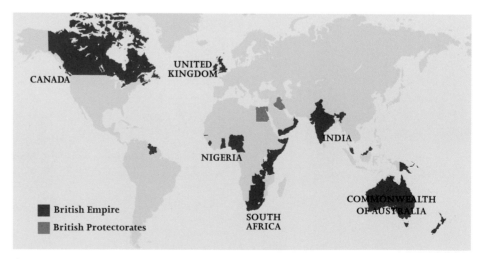

△ By the mid-1700s Britain's empire was very large. By 1763 Britain had won most of France's territory in North America. This shows the extent of the empire in 1821.

△ During the 1600s, British ships transported some 75,000 African slaves to Britain and the Americas. The slaves usually traveled in such terrible conditions that many died on the voyage.

△ St Edward's Crown is the official crown of the British king or queen. The crown was regarded as a symbol of the British empire, and India was sometimes called the "jewel" in Britain's crown.

▷ Fur trappers in North America. By 1740 the number of British colonists in North America was approaching one million. Furs and other valuable goods from the colonies, such as tobacco, timber, and grain, were sold throughout Europe.

General Wolfe

British general James Wolfe brought French power in North America to an end. Wolfe's troops attacked and seized Quebec, the most important town in French Canada, in 1759. Wolfe himself died before the battle of Quebec ended.

The slave trade

One of the most valuable cargoes was slaves, who were captured in Africa and carried across the Atlantic to work in the New World. Although started by Spanish and Portuguese settlers in America, the slave trade was controlled by British merchants from around 1600. By the end of the 1700s Britain had transported a staggering total of 2.5 million slaves. Slave labor played a huge part in the increase in sugar, tobacco, rice, and cotton growing in America, allowing many British traders to become very wealthy.

Control of India

The most successful of the trading posts set up on the Indian coast were run by the English East India Company and their close rivals, the French. India became a vital staging post on the trade route to China. By the 1720s, however, India had become an unstable country without a central ruler. The Europeans began to fight each other for power in the north. Under Robert Clive, the British won an important series of battles against French and Indian forces.

INDEX